Kindle Paperwhite

Congratulations on purchasing your very own Kindle Paperwhite. In this short collection, you will learn all of the necessary features to properly operate your new e-reader. If a feature doesn't seem to be available because of your residence or country, please visit http://www.kindle.com/support to learn more.

In this guidebook, users will learn about product specifications, getting started, basics including keyboard and WiFi networks, how to use the Kindle Store, how to navigate and read materials, and even advanced features and general maintenance. Be sure to refer to the table of contents for any specific piece of information.

Join our newsletter for FREE book promotions and updates on
our latest books!

www.grassrootbooks.com/newsletter

Product Specifications

Display: 6-inch diagonal XGA display (758 x 1024 pixels, 16 level gray scale)

Size: 6.7 inches by 4.6 inches by 0.36 inches (169 mm by 117 mm by 9.16 mm)

Weight: 7.5 – 7.8 ounces depending on Wi-Fi or Wi-Fi plus 3G

Storage: 2GB internal storage, or 1GB storage for user

Power: AC adapter sold separately and rechargeable lithium polymer battery

Connectivity: USB 2.0 (micro-B connector)

Operating Temperature: 32 F to 95 F (0 to 35C)

Storage Temperature: 14F to 113F (-10C to 45C)

Wi-Fi: 802.11 b/g/n

Table of Contents

1. Introduction to E-Readers

The Kindle Paperwhite is essential for avid e-readers. After the release of the Kindle Fire, it was within the realms of possibility for Amazon to leave its initial book lovers in order to focus on all of the advanced features of the Kindle Fire. Rather than picking up and leaving lifelong patrons in the dust, Kindle developed the Paperwhite—an ideal device for nostalgic book works and those just learning to read.

In the battle for the head honcho tablet, the Kindle Paperwhite doesn't compare with iPads and the Samsung Galaxy Note (it leaves that fight to its older brother, the Kindle Fire). In the world of e-readers, however, the Kindle Paperwhite battles the B & N Nook GlowLight and even the Amazon Kindle Touch for best e-reader.

The Nook and Paperwhite both have sleek, front-lit screens, ideal for reading in situations with little or no lighting. In terms of actual display, however, the Paperwhite actually has 62% more pixels per square inch than the other two devices. In terms of battery life, studies are rated at half hour reading per day with the usage of the front life. In this respect, the Kindle Paperwhite and Kindle Touch are both said to last eight weeks while the Nook Glowlight only lasts four weeks. All three devices weigh about the same and have similar size screens. The final reasons why the Kindle Paperwhite takes the cake comes down to 3G connectivity, X-Ray and Time to Read. The X-Ray feature is a content analysis feature that actually tracks story elements or even characters throughout a novel. Time to Read compares previous reading to remaining chapters and analyzes when a reader when finish the book, which is ideal for knowing when to download a new book and how long books will last.

Registering the Kindle Paperwhite

If a tablet was purchased online from a specific Amazon account, it will already be registered to that buyer. Tap the Home button and check the Amazon username in the upper left corner to verify the buyer name. If the desired username is not present and the tablet reads a previous owner or reads My Kindle, it is necessary to register the device as a new owner.

Step-by-Step Instructions

After making the purchase, the first step is to turn on the Kindle Paperwhite. A series of screens will emerge that help owners set up and register the device. This is the point that is essential for users to connect to a Wi-Fi network in order to properly register the device with Amazon.

- In the Connect to a Network list, use the touchscreen capabilities to tap onto an available network. The Kindle Paperwhite will connect to the network and then users can choose the appropriate

Time Zone. In some cases, users may have to enter a password to connect to a Wi-Fi network.

- Tap Select a Time Zone from the available list and then click Continue. For those in countries other than the United States, tap More for a larger list. After making a selection, use the Back button in the bottom-left corner to return to the Time Zone screen.

- Once the Register Your Kindle screen appears, current Amazon account users can enter account information, an e-mail address and a password in the fields provided. Users can deselect the Show Password box so that the password doesn't appear while typing to make sure no unintended viewers see the password.

- For those without an account, click New to Amazon to create an Account link. This link will move into the Create an Amazon Account screen. Enter information including name, e-mail address and password before pressing Continue.

- Finally, users must complete the registration. Some users will want to read the terms of registration. The next step is to tap the button that says, By Registering, You Agree to All of the Terms Found Here. After reading the registration, tap the Close button to return to the registration screen. Finally, tap Register. A final screen appears saying Welcome to Kindle Paperwhite that includes the user's name. There is also another option in case the Kindle is not registered to the correct user that says Not Your Name. Click to change if necessary.

At this point, the Kindle Paperwhite will update itself to the latest version. When the download finishes, tap the Get Started Now button to view more quick tips.

How to Deregister a Kindle

For those new Kindle owners that bought their device from a previous customer or received used, there are options to deregister a Kindle Paperwhite. In order to remove current settings, tap on Settings and then click More. Click More once again and then click on the My Account option. In this menu, click Deregister. This will delete prior credentials from the previous owner.

Managing a Kindle Account

After registering or adding an account to the Kindle Paperwhite, it's time to manage the account through the Amazon website.

By clicking on the Your Account option, users can sign in to the Amazon website. On the left column, users can then tap the Your Kindle link to move to the next step. On this page, users will be able to view a listing of eBooks regarding their particular account. Within these options, Kindle Paperwhite users can view other types of Kindle products that can be downloaded from the page. Examples include books, magazines and documents.

Under the Kindle Payment Settings option, users can add or remove payment types within their Kindle account. It's vital to have a valid card when making a purchase.

2. Kindle Controls

The section below describes the steps needed to operate the Kindle Paperwhite. Important features include the Power Button and the Micro-USB Port, among others.

Power Button

The power button is located on the bottom of the device, next to the USB outlet. To turn the device on, simply press the power button. To turn the device off, press and hold the same button for at least seven seconds. The screen will go blank when it's time to release the button.

The Kindle Paperwhite automatically goes into a sleep mode after a few moments of inactivity; similar to a screensaver on a computer. Sleep mode uses no battery. To jumpstart into the sleep mode, press and release the power button. The tablet also wakes by pressing the same power button. If the device seems to be unresponsive, press and hold the power button for twenty seconds to completely restart the Kindle Paperwhite.

Micro-USB Port

Every Kindle comes with a USB cable for charging the battery and transferring files. For those who wish to charge the device from an outlet, an AC adapter is sold separately that plugs into the same port. When charging, a lightning bolt appears where the battery icon usually resides, at the top of the Home screen. With an AC adapter, charging only takes around four hours. Charging with the USB should also only take four hours but it's possible for this to vary due to different types of hardware available; meaning various computers and other electronics.

For removing the device from Windows software, right click on the "Safely Remove Software" option on the task bar. For removing the Kindle from a Mac OS X, drag the icon into the trash or simply click the Eject option. The device is now safe to be removed or users can leave it attached for additional battery charge. Once the battery is fully charged, remove the device and feel free to begin exploring.

Status Indicator

Heading the Home screen, or available at anytime by tapping the toolbar, status indicators inform users about various activities happening within the device.

Wireless Status

Some models contain the Amazon Whispernet feature that wirelessly delivers content to the tablet on the go or in the home. Other models even include 3G connectivity. These features are displayed within the Wi-Fi symbol.

When connected to a Wi-Fi signal, an icon appears that resembles a quarter of a slice of a pie as three horizontal lines bend into a half circle. When using a 3G signal, the symbol appears as a row of dominos increasing in height from left to right. For both of these signals, full black bars represent a strong signal, similarly to most cell phones. When there are white bars present, the signal is lower. When an airplane signal appears, the device is in Airplane Mode.

Configuring Wireless Settings

Also within the Settings menu, located at the top right of the screen, users can choose a wireless network. By switching Wi-Fi to On, the device will automatically scan the area for a wireless signal. By tapping on a Wi-Fi network, users can join the network and begin using the Internet. Some networks require a password and the password option will pop up after clicking on the selected network. Passwords must be acquired from the owner of the wireless router, whether this individual is a homeowner or business employee. To enter the address, simply click within the text box and a keyboard will appear. By tapping the Show password checkbox, users can see the letters that are being keyed in. Otherwise, it's safer to not check this option and keep the password hidden from wandering eyes. After keying in the password, simply tap Connect and let the tablet connect with the selected network.

Once the device has connected to a network, there are further details that can be adjusted on the tablet. To change default settings, tap on the network name to see a status, along with link speed, signal strength and security options. Users can also examine the IP address for any networking problems that may arise from the router.

Under the Advanced Settings, Kindle Paperwhite owners can choose to Use static IP, which is useful for those with frequent router problems at home or who suffer from problems in frequent Wi-Fi hotspots. Several options, including IP address specifications are available. Users can also adjust Subnet Mask and choose between DNS numbers. This portion allows for users to Add Networks, which is crucial for connecting to those networks that are undetected or hidden for whatever reason. For this to be done, users must have a correct Network SSID, which will depend on various security types. There are six options available that range from Open to WPA2 EAP. From here, click Save to connect.

For those who connect to a large number of wireless networks, this can result in a long list of networks to make reconnecting quick and easy. To reduce the list, simply tap on any of the networks within the list and then tap Forget.

Battery Status

This indicator resembles a double-A battery on turned sidways. The black area in the center signifies the strength of the battery. An important fact to remember is that a weak Wi-Fi signal users more battery than a strong signal. This occurs because the device is constantly searching for signal, causing a strain on the battery.

Maintaining Battery Life

Because the Kindle Paperwhite is a portable device, it relies on a rechargeable battery for power supply. A full charge can generally last a day but the power life span is shortened with frequent usage. Perhaps the largest power requirement is when using Amazon Instant Video to stream movies or television shows. However, there are ways to preserve battery life.

The first step is to make sure the Kindle Paperwhite is being charged correctly. One way is to attach the Kindle Paperwhite to a computer by using a USB chord, but this is not the most effective way. It's best to use the wall charger that comes with the device and allowing for the tablet to have a full recharge that will take a few hours. This should be done once a week and the tablet should be left to charge for at least four hours.

For those who have the brightness at full level or who may be using full volume, the battery will seem to drain quickly. It's important to keep these settings at low and appropriate levels. Another issue is within the wireless network. When the Kindle Paperwhite is having problems connecting with a weak connection, the battery will be drained. When using the device in weak signal areas, it's a good idea to disable the Wi-Fi to save battery. In addition, battery is also drained when downloading or syncing large files. Generally, the Kindle Paperwhite battery life should last up to eight hours when reading and at least seven for video playback (as long as Wi-Fi is disabled).

Activity Status

Arriving in the top-left corner of the screen, this appears when the tablet is connecting to a network, downloading content, opening a large file, loading a web page or syncing items.

3. Using the Kindle Paperwhite Screen

By tapping within any areas that requires text, such as the Search feature, a keyboard will appear at the bottom of the screen. Type in your necessary words or phrases and continue to the next action. There is also a 123!? option for numbers and symbols. To return, tap this same button, which will change to an ABC option when users are in the number and symbols keyboard. Some users will find it difficult to type on the keyboard when the device is vertical because the keyboard will be smaller than when it is horizontal.

For other languages, go to the Settings page and select Device Options. From this page, click Language and Dictionaries. When users add multiple keyboards, a Globe key will appear along with the 123 and ABC options that come standard. For other diacritics or special characters, hold an individual letter on the keyboard until further options appear on the screen. For example, changing an n into an ñ.

Touchscreen Areas

For effortless page turns, the EasyReach feature is readily available. Users can tap almost anywhere on the screen to turn to the next page of an e-book. Tap the left side to go back a page and the right to move forward. Readers can also change pages by swiping across the screen. After all, the device was created for ease of use and overall learnability.

Toolbars

The EasyReach feature also allows users to tap the top area of the touchscreen in order to show a toolbar. When the toolbar option appears, users can go back to the Home screen, go back a page, adjust brightness, visit the Kindle store, search within the text or display more Menu options. These options are somewhat self-explanatory but further detail is presented below:

Home Button: Resembling a small home, this button takes users back to the original home page; to a list of stored content on the Kindle Paperwhite.

Back Button: This left-facing arrow takes users back a single frame to help users retrace their steps or search for similar content. This is similar to Back buttons on most web browsers.

Screen Light: A light bulb icon; a horizontal line will appear for users to slide their finger across in order to change light settings. For those trying to save battery, keep the screen at a dimmer level by moving it closer to the "-" and away from the "+." To make the screen brighter, do the exact opposite.

Kindle Store: By tapping on the shopping cart icon, users will be escorted into the Kindle store, as long as they have a 3G connection or are within a Wi-Fi hot spot. Inside this online store, users can search for and/or purchase various types of media for the tablet.

Search Button: This magnifying glass icon allows for users to search for content within the selected text on the screen. By touching the left side of the Search field, readers can choose whether they are searching within This Book, My Items, Kindle Store, Dictionary, or Wikipedia. This is ideal for students and teachers or anyone wanting to learn more about a work of literature.

Menu Button: These three horizontal lines represent the Menu. Contextually, this button changes depending on which area of the device the user is currently using. For example, when reading a book, menu options include Portrait or Landscape Mode, Sync to Furthest Page Read, Book Description, Add Bookmark, View Notes & Marks, Reading Progress and About the Author (this feature depends on support from author profile).

Secondary Toolbar

When reading a book, a secondary toolbar appears with four more options. These options are listed below:

Text Option: Listed as "Aa," this feature allows for users to change the font size, typeface, margins, font or typeface.

Go To Option: Presented as "Go To," this button may include Beginning, Page or Location or Chapter Titles depending on the type of book being read.

X-Ray Option: This feature allows for users to explore the "bones" or structure with a single touch. Meaning, users can search within the passages to explore specific ideas, characters, historical figures or locations. Unfortunately, not all books contain this feature, nor do all countries.

Share Option: Tap this option to share thoughts with other readers. More information will be presented on this subject regarding linking social networks.

4. Security on the Kindle Paperwhite

Because tablets can be connected to the Internet and may hold personal data along with credit card information, it's important to keep the Kindle Paperwhite protected. The lock screen can be assigned an encrypted password and parental controls can also be given to keep children from accessing the device without an adult.

Password for Lock Screen

When the Kindle Paperwhite is turned on or awakened from sleep mode, the Lock Screen appears. In this standby mode, there are default settings randomly displayed. This feature protects the Kindle Paperwhite from accidentally being turned on or from any of the apps running unexpectedly that may run down power on the tablet. There are two types of lock screen variations available. To change between these options, visit Settings and then click More, followed by tapping Security. From here, tap Lock Screen Password and decide between Tap or Drag to combine a password of four characters for the tablet.

Password options are flexible and can be composed of letters, character and numbers. After choosing and confirming a password, users can test the password by tapping the power button and switching it to standby, followed by tapping the power button again to wake the tablet. In order to disable a password, the password must be entered beforehand. It's important to know that when a password is entered incorrectly four times, the Kindle Paperwhite must be reset.

Credential Storage

For those with Microsoft Exchange-based accounts, there is a Credential Storage option available within the Security Screen. This does not apply to most users but for those that do need such a feature, the network administrator is necessary for configuration. Within the Security Screen, tap on Install Secure Credentials, Set Credential Storage Password and Use Secure Credentials. To reset any of these options, tap Clear Credential Storage.

Setting Parental Controls

Because children are as attracted to electronics as adults, it's vital to have a safety lock on all tablets. Some websites are inappropriate for children and because of the possibility of having a credit card linked with various apps, it's wise to protect the Kindle Paperwhite from children who may wish to explore the device. By tapping Settings, then More, then Parental controls, users can decide whether to toggle the button to On or Off. This feature protects the tablet from both children and potential thieves who many tamper with the tablet. Using Parental Controls helps to restrict certain purchases and keep others from visiting inappropriate websites or accessing content that should not be accessed. After activating the

Parental Control, the device will only be able to be used for those who know the secure password.

Updating and Resetting the Kindle Paperwhite

Whether users are purchasing a used Kindle or giving one as a gift, there is an option to reset the Kindle Paperwhite for new owners. Some may wish to simply update the Kindle Paperwhite while others may want to completely reset the device.

For those who wish to change an account, this requires deregistering the tablet. To deregister a Kindle Paperwhite, simply tap on Settings, then More, then tap on My Account. From here, users can deregister the previous account and begin to assign a new account holder. New Amazon accounts can be keyed in or completely new accounts can be created. It's possible to then sync the tablet with previously purchased content and media. Please review the opening chapters of this guidebook to find out more about how to properly set up a Kindle Paperwhite.

It's important to remember that when changing owners, all of the previous data that has been downloaded or synced from another account will be removed from the tablet. This will not erase data from the Cloud, merely the tablet. To find out which forms of media are on the tablet, click on Settings, then More, then My Account and finally, tap Device. This will display all data held on the device. Storage is divided between Application Storage and Internal Storage where the Application portion holds 1.17

GB and the Internal holds 5.36 GB. It's a good idea to occasionally check this data to find out what is being held on the device and what can be deleted. New users who do not want to reset the Kindle can check here to decide what to keep and what to erase.

For new owners to fully experience the personal touch of the Kindle Paperwhite, it's best to Reset the device. In the Device window, move down and tap the option that reads, Reset to Factory Defaults. Since this step is so detrimental to the device, a confirmation will arise to confirm this is truly the option the user wishes to perform. Also, the device will need at least forty percent battery to perform this feature. Despite the severity of the action, the reset is a fairly quick procedure. For those who think there may be additional data on the device, they can simply plug the tablet to a computer using a USB and manually erase any media within the Video, Music, Books, Pictures or Documents folders on the Kindle Paperwhite.

5. Kindle Paperwhite

Troubleshooting

When problems arise, it's important to solve them quickly for a quick-loading, efficient tablet. Sometimes, the device may have some lag time between screens or with certain apps or games. Usually, this is involved with poor battery management, which can be solved by providing the Kindle Paperwhite with a full charge. However, there are several other tips to remember for the most efficient tablet.

Restarting the Tablet

On the rare occasion that the tablet locks up, an app fails or the tablet freezes, it's important to respond accordingly. If users are unable to return to the Newsstand for any reason, it may be time to turn it off for a moment. There are two ways to restart the device.

- Before taking any action, it's important to decide whether or not the tablet has enough energy for a reboot. Sometimes, the tablet may be performing some process in the background, which is causing the battery to run low. If the battery is low, it's a good idea to charge the battery for half an hour before running a Hard Reset. If possible, perform the normal reset procedure by holding down the power button until the Shut Down button appears.

- If the device is completely frozen, the only way to reset the Kindle Paperwhite is to hold down the power button for at least twenty seconds. From here, simply turn the tablet back on and the issue should be resolved.

Synchronization Issues

One particular frustrating problem comes from syncing books from the Amazon Cloud to the Kindle Paperwhite. This may happen when various Kindle devices are assigned to one Amazon account—whether there are several tablets or various smartphones registered. One issue will resolve with missing pages from a downloaded book. Usually, missing pages are in fault due the book's author. If a user encounters this issue, it's ideal to Report the book on the Kindle Store product listing.

Other issues that arise from improper book downloading can be fixed by restarting the device or simply disconnecting and then reconnecting the Wi-Fi. Other problems that may occur happen when opening a book on the tablet. This can be fixed by opening the Books list and long tapping the book before finally selecting the Remove from Device option. From here, click the Cloud view and tap the book again to re-download. If this problem continues, Restart the device.

Lost Password

For those who have decided to secure a device with a screen lock password, it's possible to occasionally forget the code. For a lost password, the only option is to restore the device to the original factory settings. If this happens, the device will delete all personal data and content until it is properly registered again. From here, users can download former books from the Amazon Cloud. If a new password is assigned, make sure to make it memorable.

6. Buying Books in the Kindle Store

Like any Kindle, the main reason for purchasing a tablet is for the reading capabilities. In order to get started, it's crucial to have a wireless network connection, an Amazon account with a credit or debit card linked to the account.

By tapping on the Books option in the virtual bookshelf on the Kindle home screen, account holders can be reading a best seller within a few seconds. From this point, the next step is to tap the Store option so the tablet moves into the browser and displays the Kindle store. Within the Store, there are currently over one million titles to choose from.

After finding a specific magazine or book, customers can use the Buy Now With One Click button to make an instant purchase. It's important to activate an account before using this option.

Finding Free Books to Read

Customers are not merely limited to buying books thanks to actions from Amazon. Many titles can actually be found for free to customers who are willing to look. Most classic books from historic authors can be found for free online.

One way to find free books is to use the search tool within the Kindle Store. However, this option often leads to customers searching for hours with little luck. By searching the Internet, customers will find that there are several websites that announce when new eBooks are free within the Kindle Store. Try a search such as "free books Kindle" that uses key words to find free books.

Searching the Newsstand

After pressing the Home button, users will be moved to the Newsstand, which is a virtual bookshelf where books and apps are located. By swiping left or right with a finger or stylus, users can scroll through shelves of materials. By using this carousel-like browser, users can find any item they may consider using. If a certain material isn't found immediately, users can browse other shelves below or use the search tool at the top of the tablet by keying in a key word or phrase.

Tablet for Book Lovers

Because of the book-lover chromosome in the DNA of the Kindle Paperwhite, the Newsstand is vital for holding books. The Newsstand provides a way for book lovers to find recent and familiar titles at any time, even on the go. On the Newsstand or Books menu, users can find titles to store on the device or in the Amazon cloud. Within the Cloud, books can be sorted alphabetically by Author, Recent or Title.

In order to launch a book for the first time, it's important to follow two steps. First, a user must download the publication by giving the book a single tap. Next, the user can click the cover illustration after the eBook has downloaded and presented itself on the tablet. Any book on the Kindle Paperwhite can be moved to Favorites for a quick find. To do so, simply find the item and tap and hold to display the menu. On the menu, click the Add to Favorites feature to move the item into the Newsstand.

Reading Books and Documents

After opening a book on the tablet, turning a page is as simple as swiping a finger or stylus from left to right, or by tapping on the screen. To go back to the menu, users can tap on the bottom edge of the screen. From this point, the Home button and Back button will be revealed, along with Font Size options. Readers can also jump through the book to specific parts and there is also an Annotation button for readers to add notes or thoughts throughout the piece. In the menu, a Search tool is useful for finding specific phrases or sentences. These two features are great for students conducting research on historic works of literature.

While reading, there is a progress bar to let readers know which page they are currently on and where they are in the book. This bar also includes a slider that allows readers to move throughout the book.

In the top right corner, readers can find a grey bookmark. By tapping this page while reading, users can return to that particular page at any time during the reading. This is also helpful for those conducting research on a book.

Besides Kindle eBooks, there are other forms of documents that can be read on a Kindle Paperwhite. Other forms have less menu options but these documents can still be read by using the pinch-to-zoom gesture, ideal for documents in the PDF format. On most documents, a double tap also zooms. Documents can be read in formats including Kindle Format 8, Kindle Mobi (.azw), txt, pdf, mobi, and prc. All of these documents can be enjoyed in full color on the LCD screen. Books and magazines in these formats can be copied to the Kindle Paperwhite by using a USB cable.

Using the Search Feature

When using the Search feature outside of the book, the tool helps Kindle Paperwhite owners search for books in any format, title or topic within the tablet. To use this feature, users simply tap into the Search box, which opens the Search page and gives results in the same area.

The Search feature can also be used to search the Internet by tapping on the Web button in the top right corner and keying in a search term. By tapping on the Library button, the search will then move back to focus on items in the tablet. Besides books and documents, apps and games can also be searched for by using this feature.

While reading a book, there is another search feature for users of the Kindle Paperwhite. While in book view, readers can use the Search feature by tapping the magnifying glass Search button. It's important to type a long and accurate search phrase in the bar. To find the best results, it may take some time.

Removing Books

Despite the large amount of space on the Kindle Paperwhite, users will still decide to delete books purchased from the Kindle store that they have already read or perhaps didn't enjoy. Removing a book from the reader is quite simple.

To begin, open the Books section and find the title that needs to be removed. Use the Search tool if necessary. After finding the specific book, tap and hold until the Remove from Device option appears. From here, the book will disappear from the Kindle Paperwhite, but it will still remain in the account of the Amazon cloud.

Using the Keyboard

Once a Kindle Paperwhite owner understands the basics of the gestures, it's time to engage the keyboard. The tablet is stocked with a software keyboard that displays on the screen; unlike previous Kindles that featured a physical keyboard.

Generally, the keyboard is hidden and only reveals itself when information is necessary. The keyboard automatically appears when emails or forms are opened or when connected to Wi-Fi. The keyboard also appears if the Search box is opened or whenever a user taps within a text field.

When the keyboard opens, a standard QWERTY keyboard appears, along with a series of numbers from 1 to 0. Numbers are entered by either tapping the 123!? to the left of the Space bar, which will display a secondary keyboard to replace the first. This secondary keyboard will feature numbers and various forms of punctuation. There is also a third keyboard option available that displays math symbols. Pressing the ABC key can bring the main keyboard back.

Typing is as simple as using any keyboard, although the feel of the flat screen will be different at first. Using the backspace key on the top right corner of the keyboard can erase mistakes. The cursor can also be dragged to various points of the text by moving it with the finger on the top portion of the screen.

Copy and paste features are also available on the Kindle Paperwhite. In order to select a word or phrase, users simply double tap on a selected word and tap it once more to display the Edit text menu. Within the Edit text menu, the Cut and Copy options appear. To paste or copy text, users long tap the text field and the Paste option will appear. There is also an Input Method on this same menu that allows for users to switch between the Kindle Paperwhite keyboard and alternatives keyboards that can be purchased within the Amazon App Store.

Some users find the keyboard to be difficult because of the size of the individual keys and the unfamiliarity when compared to a typical computer keyboard. In both forms of the keyboard (portrait and landscape), nearly half of the screen is devoted to the keyboard. Because the screen is so large, some users have trouble seeing the other half of the screen. By using the scroll feature, users can move the non-keyboard part of the screen to see more or close the keyboard button by clicking a close option in the lower left corner of the screen. When the phrase or word is complete, the user simply presses the submit key in the lower right corner.

Amazon Prime

Similar to other rental or streaming organizations, Amazon Prime is a service that provides entertainment in the form of streaming and shipping. For a flat membership fee, Amazon provides Amazon Instant Video, which streams select television shows and films directly onto the Kindle or computer. In 2011, this extended to Kindle's Lending Library, where users can borrow a number of great titles with no due date.

Lending Books

For a period of up to two weeks, Kindle Books can be loaned to other readers. The borrower does not even need to own a Kindle to take up this enticing offer. Not all books are lendable, but users can determine which books are by looking in the product details to see if lending is enabled. To lend a book, simply check to see if the book is lendable and then click Loan this book in the Actions menu. With Amazon Prime, there are over 270,000 books for Kindle owners to borrow from for free and with no due dates. This includes all of the *Harry Potter* books and over 100 current and previous *New York Times* Best Sellers.

7. Installing and Launching Apps

After setting up the Kindle Paperwhite, users can spend leisure time enjoying books and magazines on a high speed, full color display. Besides the basic reading materials, users can install and launch apps from the Amazon App Store, which is an online marketplace for the device. The App Store can be reached from any wireless connection but there are some international restrictions.

Installing New Apps

Finding new apps is simple. Tap on Apps and then click on Store to browse available selections. When users see an app of interest, they can tap on the app to open a description page. From here, Kindle Paperwhite users can find out details about the product, along with screenshots and even reviews from other users. In addition, the description page also gives recommendations for similar apps in the same genre.

After choosing an app, the next step is to install the app. Like downloading books, it's important to have a credit card linked to the Amazon account. View the price list on the app or description page and then tap on the Get App option. The download will complete in the background while the progress bar will have a status bar in the foreground.

Other Resources to Download Apps

Because not all Kindle Paperwhite owners are in the United States, there are other services available to install apps and games. In order to do this, it's important to make sure the device is set up to install apps from a third party location.

In order to complete this task, Open Settings and then tap More, followed by Device. Switch Allow Installation of Applications from the default setting of Off to On. The tablet will inform the user that this action isn't safe but the choice is utterly up to owner of the device and must be done to download items from other locations.

While the Kindle Paperwhite is trying to protect itself, there are several safe options for third party downloads. One of the most popular platforms is the Opera App Store, available at apps.opera.com in the Kindle Paperwhite Browser. The Opera App Store accepts credit cards or PayPal as forms of currency to purchase apps. This platform works basically the same way by finding an app and clicking on the Download option.

After clicking the Download option, tap the Menu button in the middle of the browser toolbar and then select Downloads. From this point, there is a progress bar available to see the progress of the download. After the download completes, the user can tap on the completed app and begin the installation procedure. From here, there are more specific instructions set as guidelines.

Other resources such as andappstore.com, slideme.org and m.getjar.com work similarly. As a general guideline, it's wise not to install any apps that aren't currently available within the official Google Play store or the Amazon App Store.

Uninstalling Apps

When an app is no longer useful or there is another reason the user wants to delete the app, uninstalling is quick and easy. By opening the Apps screen, users can long tap the app to be removed until a menu appears that allows users to Remove from Device. For those who wish to remove the app from the Newsstand rather than the entire tablet, this can be completed by tapping and holding until the menu says, Remove from Carousel, keeping it on the tablet and out of the way.

8. Collecting and Managing Content

Offering a variety of books, newspapers, magazines, games and content, the Kindle Store truly has something for everyone. In order to browse the content, tap the top of the screen to display the toolbar and then tap the Shopping Cart option. Other menu options also read Shop Kindle Store in various menus.

Once inside the store, navigation is quite simple. Touch any area of interest and swipe left or right, or up and down to move throughout the virtual store. Search for titles or browse within categories for quick results. Users can also check best sellers list, read customer reviews, download samples and find personal recommendations.

A one-click payment option is prepared for those ready to make a purchase. The selected item will then be downloaded directly to the device to read, watch or play. Newspapers, blogs and magazines are available for download before they are available for print in many cases. The only necessity the device requires is Wi-Fi or 3G connectivity and then most features can be downloaded in less than a minute. The Kindle Paperwhite can also be synchronized to previous purchases from a user's account.

Cloud and Device Storage

Materials that are not downloaded directly to the device are stored within the Cloud. To view content stored within the Cloud, tap the Cloud option located in the upper left corner of the Home screen.

For content stored within the tablet, click the Device option. For those about to go offline for whatever reason, visit the Cloud and download content directly to the device in order to read or view in offline mode. To do so, tap Cloud and choose the item or items to download. Items can be canceled by tapping on the title during a download. Downloaded items can then be opened from the Home screen. Keeping the tablet in Airplane Mode and offline will also help save battery life.

Removing Items

For those users with too much content, some items must be deleted from the device to clear up space. Simply tap and hold on the name or cover of the item to be deleted. A digital box will appear that allows users to Remove from Device. The content will remain in the cloud but will no longer be on the actual tablet. However, files transferred from a USB cable will be permanently deleted.

Understanding Periodicals

Back issues of newspaper or magazines are stored within the "Periodicals: Back Issues" section on the device. After seven issues, older content will automatically be deleted to invite new content on the device. When an issue features the "Expiring" tag next to it, the issue will be deleted periodically.

Keeping an "Expiring" issue can be done one of two ways: Press and hold the name of the issue on the home screen. Select Keep This Issue when the digital box appears. Inside the issue, select the Menu button and tap Keep This Issue.

Kindle Library Management

Since the tablet can hold thousands of digital books, newspapers, blogs, magazines, and personal documents, it's important to understand how to navigate through all of this content. Begin by tapping the Home button to examine the amount of free space available. From here, tap the Menu option and then Settings. Finally, select Device Info. Content is stored by most Recent. The order can be changed within the header. Items within the Cloud can also be managed from this screen.

For those who wish to filter by type, tap My Items within the Home screen. Content can be filtered as All Items, Books, Periodicals, Docs, and Active Content. For more information on any individual item, visit the Home screen and press and hold the particular item's cover. This Menu that appears will include Add to Collection, Go To…, Search This Book, Book Description, View Notes & Marks and even Remove from Device.

Start Collecting

For those users who store a great deal of content,

collections can be created for easier access. Collections can hold as many items as a user wishes to store. Items can also be added to various collections similar to songs within a playlist. Follow these steps to create a new collection:

1. Tap Menu on the Home screen
2. Choose Create New Collection
3. When the keyboard appears, type in a name for the new selection and then select OK (periodicals and blogs are not options for creating collections)
4. Click the checkbox on an item's title to add it to the collection and then tap the Done feature

Items can be removed or added after creating a collection by selecting the Menu button in a collection, followed by Add/Remove items.

9. Reading Documents on the Kindle

The Kindle Paperwhite uses a high-resolution display known as electronic ink, or E Ink. With this reflective technology, users can even use the device in bright sunlight. Displaying ink particles electronically, E Ink uses ink like books or newspapers. When turning pages, a single "flash" may appear on the screen. This occurs because the E Ink is updating and trying to give readers smooth page turns and quick features. Uses can adjust the page refreshment by tapping Menu, Reading Options and then the Page Refresh feature.

Customize Text Display

For quick adjustments to the appearance of books and periodicals, tap the top of the screen to bring up a toolbar once inside the periodical. Tap the Text button that will appear as an "Aa" and a digital box will come to the surface. This box allows for users to change typeface, size, line spacing or even margins. Some books even contain a Publisher font option to view fonts embedded from the original publisher.

Document Interactions

Unlike a paper book or document, the Kindle provides features far more advanced than previous materials. Besides being able to highlight or add notes, users can create specific bookmarks and look up words in the dictionary instantaneously by simply pressing and holding any word in question. Default dictionaries come standard, but some users wish to change these settings:

1. At Home, tap Menu, then Settings
2. Select Device Options, then Language and Dictionaries
3. Select Dictionary, then choose dictionary language (if there is an arrow pointing right, there are several options available)
4. Use the radio button to select a particular dictionary

Search: Tap the top of the screen and then select the magnifying glass. Kindle Paperwhite owners can search within My Items, Kindle Store, Dictionary and Wikipedia.

Highlights and Notes: Press and hold any particular text to add highlights or notes. Drag your finger across the touchscreen to select the phrase. When selecting a single word, options include Show Full Definition, Highlight, and More. For addition settings, tap More. It's even possible to report errors in the content from here.

When selecting multiple words or a full sentence, the dialog box appears as Share, Add Note, Highlight, and More. Additional actions in the more category now include Wikipedia, translations and errors within content.

After making notes, these notes will appear as superscript

numbers along with the previous text. Tap on the number to view any particular note. If other users have highlighted or made notes throughout the book, distracting a reader, this reader can hide these by selecting Settings in the Home menu, followed by Reading Options and then the Popular Highlights settings.

Bookmarks: Bookmarks are automatically saved thanks to Amazon's Whispersync technology. To add additional bookmarks, select Add Bookmark or tap on the icon in the upper right corner. Digitally, the top corner folds itself down to represent a saved page. To delete any particular bookmark, tap this icon again and choose the Delete Bookmark option within the menu. Bookmarks, notes and highlights are grouped together within the My Clippings section.

X-Ray: This feature allows for users to explore the "bones" or structure with a single touch. Meaning, users can search within the passages to explore specific ideas, characters, historical figures or locations. Unfortunately, not all books contain this feature, nor do all countries.

Viewing Options

The Kindle Paperwhite comes with various options within the reading progress. Options include location within a book, page numbers, time left in chapter, time left in book, percentage of content read and actual page numbers (for some books). Since Kindle books can be ready on several devices, it's vital to have a form of locating aspects within a book, similar to page numbers in a paperback.

For those wondering how the time left features work, the Reading Progress uses a specific algorithm to estimate the time it will take to finish a chapter based off previous and current reading speeds. To view a page number, tap the top screen and find the toolbar. The current location, page number total number of pages and percentage of content read will appear at the bottom of the screen. A row of dots also appear, showing how far a reader it into the book, displayed as bold dots.

10. Sending and Receiving Emails

When tablets hit the market, businessmen and students were excited to have a portable emailing device, with sending and receiving capabilities. These emails can also have attachments that even include photos. By providing email functions, the Kindle Paperwhite has the same capabilities of other tablets and smartphones. This is ideal for keeping in touch with friends and co-workers at any moment and being able to respond all hours of the day. The Kindle Paperwhite can access personal and corporate email accounts. Unlike former devices, the Kindle Paperwhite has complete email configuration for accounts like Gmail, Hotmail and other accounts. In the Advanced settings, users can configure the Kindle Paperwhite to work with any email account to keep in touch with all friends, family and coworkers.

Set Up, Collect and Send

After properly setting up the Silk Browser, users can load emails. In the Apps screen, the Kindle Paperwhite has an Email app available that can support several accounts for those with multiple emails or for anyone sharing a tablet with family or spouse. After launching this app, the user will be asked to key in an account name along with a password. Most of the settings are available through a default method but users can change any settings by tapping Menu and then Accounts. In order to switch between accounts, there is a switch in the drop down menu in the upper left corner of the screen within the email app.

After keying in the correct information, email messages will appear in the inbox. By tapping on any of these messages, users can read and reply to any particular message. Messages can also be forwarded just like using a computer. In order to send a message, simply tap on the Compose button in the menu of the email app and type the email address of whoever is meant to receive the message. For those who wish to send multiple messages, simply tap on the Cc/Bcc button to send to any number of intended recipients. Make sure to enter a subject into the Subject line and make sure to click the Save Draft button while writing long emails that may take time to finish. After typing the message, simply tap the Attach button to add an image or file to the document being sent. Make sure to be familiar with the keyboard and typing messages from the Kindle Paperwhite will be simple. Once the message is complete, simply tap Send to mail the message to the recipient.

Additional Email Settings

For those who want more than default settings, there are options available to change the email app on the Kindle Paperwhite. One change involves the Check for messages button that rests in the middle of the menu bar on the email app. This button actually overrides default settings to allow for users to decide whether they want to manually check for messages or have message alerts. There is also a Search tool on the menu bar that allows for users to search for specific messages within the email account. There is a sorting option in the top right section of the screen that is set on Newest, but allows for users to decide how the Inbox is arranged. Other options include Sender, Subject, and Attachments.

Also on the menu button, there is a list of Contacts associated with each email account. The Kindle Paperwhite will automatically sync a user's list of contacts from their email account. The Folders button also provides users with other folders such as Outbox and Sent items. These are ideal when using a multitude of devices for email services. The Settings button gives a few more options to create a personal email experience.

After tapping on the Settings option, users can choose an Account name and decide which is used as the Default account. Within these settings, users can choose whether or not images are automatically shown in emails. By tapping on Always show images the user can choose Yes or No. Choosing No is ideal for accounts that get a great deal of spam messages. For those who wish to see images from friends but not spam, there is an option to choose images From contacts or From anyone, which helps to specify which images are received.

By tapping the Fetch new messages option, users can choose between Manually, Hourly, Every 15 minutes or Every 30 minutes to decide how often messages are checked. Kindle Paperwhite owners can also decide whether or not they wish for messages to be deleted from the tablet or from the server. The When I delete option gives two chooses that are Do not delete on server or Delete from server. Finally, users can choose standard or encrypted email collections by configuring the Incoming mail server option.

11. Advanced Kindle

Paperwhite

To customize any particular setting for the device, go to the Settings page by tapping the Menu button on the Home screen. Available settings include Airplane Mode, Wi-Fi Networks, Registration, and Device Options.

Device Options allow for users to set a passcode, set the correct time, select a language, enable Parental Controls, add various language keyboards, choose dictionaries, add personal information, personalize the device name in the upper left corner, and even view Send-to-Kindle e-mail addresses, among other options.

Device Passcode

Using a passcode allows for Kindle owners to restrict access to the device without permission. The passcode will need to be entered whenever the device is awakened from sleep mode. If the passcode is forgotten, owners must contact Kindle Customer Service.

Parental Controls

Resembling a tool chest lock, this symbol indicates that the Parental Controls have been enabled to block certain content from being seen. This feature is great for parents as it restricts access to certain aspects of the Kindle Store, content within the Cloud as well as various websites. This blocks both inappropriate content and keeps the device safe from unexpected online purchasing.

Device Time

At the top of the screen, users can check the current local time. For travelers with 3G, there is a "set automatically" feature within the Settings. To see the time while reading, simply tap the top of the touchscreen.

Personalize the Kindle Paperwhite

Manage the device name or add personal information by using the following steps:

Device Name: Change the name displayed at the top left corner of the screen.

Personal Info: Users can add personal or contact information in this field, which is useful if the tablet is ever misplaced.

Send-to-Kindle E-mail: This indicates where documents will be sent as they are being read on the device. Another positive feature is that unsupported documents will automatically be reformatted to fit the Kindle Paperwhite.

Language and Dictionaries: Select a language for the tablet or add various keyboards and languages. Also, select default or updated dictionaries.

Reading Options: Manage annotations, highlights, public notes, social networks and page refresh. All of these aspects come standard but users are invited to change any particular setting to truly make the Kindle Paperwhite a personal device.

Settings Contextual Menu

Within the Settings page, tap the Menu option for further choices. These new options include Shop Kindle Store, which directs users to the store. Update Your Kindle installs the most up-to-date software on the device (if dim, there are no further updates). Restart will restart the Kindle but will not erase any files on the tablet and can be performed by holding the power button for twenty seconds. Reset Device, however, changes the Kindle back to the original factory settings. This feature should not be performed unless properly instructed from Kindle Customer Service. It's important to back-up all content before performing this action. Device Info will display the network capability, available space, firmware version, and Wi-Fi MAC address. Legal displays all copyright and trademark materials regarding software. Finally, Sync & Check for Items syncs the device with cloud content.

Special Offers and Ads

Amazon offers a $20 fee to remove special offers from the device but it's important to understand that this does not include all ads within the Kindle Store. There will still be Editor's Picks and other ads for upcoming and new releases. One way to reduce these ads would be to use the List View rather than the Cover View, which comes down to user preference. Another way to reduce the amount of ads is to turn off the Kindle Store within the parental controls section. Some users find this annoying because they will have to visit parental controls each time they visit the store and retype in the password.

Reading Personal Documents

With the Kindle Paperwhite, it's easy to carry thousands of documents at all times. Owners and approved contacts can e-mail documents directly to the Kindle Paperwhite. In order to locate the Send-to-Kindle E-mail address, tap on the Home button and then choose Settings. From here, choose Device Options and then Personalize Your Kindle. E-mailed personal documents will be back backed up within the Kindle Library and downloadable at any moment as long as Personal Document Archiving is enabled. Users can send documents in various files including DOC, DOCX, PDF, HTML, TXT, RTF, JPEG, GIF, PNG, BMP, PRC and MOBI.

Sharing Comments through Social Networks

For those who wish to share highlights and other comments on social networks like Twitter and Facebook, the Kindle Paperwhite has the capabilities. To link social networking accounts, visit the Home screen and tap Menu and then Settings. From here, click Reading Options and then Social Networks.

After this feature has been setup, open any book and select Share from the second toolbar to share messages in any linked social network. Press and hold the text and then drag a finger across the screen to properly select the quote or phrase. This feature is not yet available in all countries.

Linking with a Computer

When the Kindle Paperwhite is first connected to a computer, it will show up as an icon as if it were an external storage unit. There will be a directory or folder entitled, "documents." From here, Kindle-compatible files can be added and these files can be copied, moved or deleted. In this mode, the device can not be used for reading.

Experimental Web Browsing

Every tablet comes with an experimental web browser allowing users to surf and view most Amazon pages smoothly. This browser supports JavaScript, SSL and cookies but not media plug-ins and Wi-Fi is necessary for most websites. To use the Web Browser, go to the Home screen and tap Menu. Next, select Experimental Browser. Upon the first viewing, there will be a list of default bookmarks of commonly used sites. For a personal touch, most users change these bookmarks by tapping on Bookmarks within the Web Browser menu.

For entering any URL, click the Search area at the top of the screen and use the onscreen keyboard for typing. There is no need to add the .com because it will be added automatically. After the page loads, tap on other links to load new pages or move throughout the Internet or drag a finger up and down or left and right to navigate on a single page. For previous pages, tap the Menu button and then History.

Web Browser Menu

Once inside the Web Browser, the Menu option includes Article Mode, Bookmarks, Bookmark this Page, History and Browser Settings. Within the Browser Settings, additional options include Clear Cookies, Clear History, Disable JavaScript, and Disable Images. Web pages actually load faster without JavaScript but this is up to the owner to decide whether or not to use or disable. For articles, there is an option to change to Article Mode that allows for users to see a different page layout.

Bookmarks

Bookmarks are automatically saved thanks to Amazon's Whispersync technology. To add additional bookmarks, select Add Bookmark or tap on the icon in the upper right corner. Tap the Remove button at the bottom of the screen to take away any unwanted bookmarks. For multiple, select unwanted URLs on the checkbox and then tap Remove.

Downloading Files

On occasion, there will be articles that users will want to read again or read later. Simply tap the downloadable file and then the Kindle Paperwhite will prompt the user to confirm that the selected document will be downloaded.

Additional Assistance

For customer service, visit the website,
http://www.kindle.com/support
for additional information, how-to videos and frequently
asked questions regarding the Kindle Paperwhite.

Maintaining the Kindle Paperwhite

Avoid all potentially wet locations including sinks, pools or
bad weather. Avoid spilling food or drink near the device.
If the tablet does manage to get wet despite best efforts,
unplug it immediately and turn off the wireless features
(Menu > Settings > enable Airplane Mode). Then, let the
device move into sleep mode. Wait for the tablet to dry
completely before trying to turn it back on. Never attempt
to dry the device by using any type of heat source such as
microwave or hair dryer. Use a soft cloth to clean the
screen and it's recommended to buy a cover to avoid
scratches or other unforeseen instances. Finally, make
sure to avoid leaving the device in extreme temperatures
of excess heat or freezing cold.

For users who engage in repetitive motions on the device,
it's possible to cause strain or discomfort in hands, arms,
shoulders or neck. If this occurs, discontinue using the
device and consult a physician for follow-up steps of
recovery. To reduce these possible risks, take frequent
breaks and avoid prolonged risk. Never use your Kindle
Paperwhite while operating a vehicle or when it is a
hazardous distraction.

GrassRootBooks.com Publishing

GrassRootBooks.com is a boutique publishing firm that specializes in publishing fiction and non-fiction Books. We have a number of high-quality works currently available on the Amazon Marketplace.

Check out our site and join our newsletter for updates on our latest books, free book promotions, and upcoming releases.

www.grassrootbooks.com/newsletter

At GrassRoot Books, we work with both accomplished and up and coming authors, partnering with talent and producing high-quality works. Check out our homepage at www.grassrootbooks.com

Copyright Note:

www.ingramcontent.com/pod-product-compliance
Lightning Source LLC
Chambersburg PA
CBHW071032050326
40689CB00014B/3617